GARFIELD'S Stupid Cupid
And Other Silly Stories

Created by
JIM DAVIS

Written by Mark Acey and Jim Kraft
Designed and Illustrated by Mike Fentz

Watermill Press

Published by Watermill Press, an imprint of Troll Associates, Inc.
No part of this book may be reproduced or utilized in any form or by any means,
electronic or mechanical, including photocopying, recording, or by any information
storage or retrieval system, without written permission from the publisher.

Printed in the United States of America.

10 9 8 7 6 5 4 3 2 1

Contents

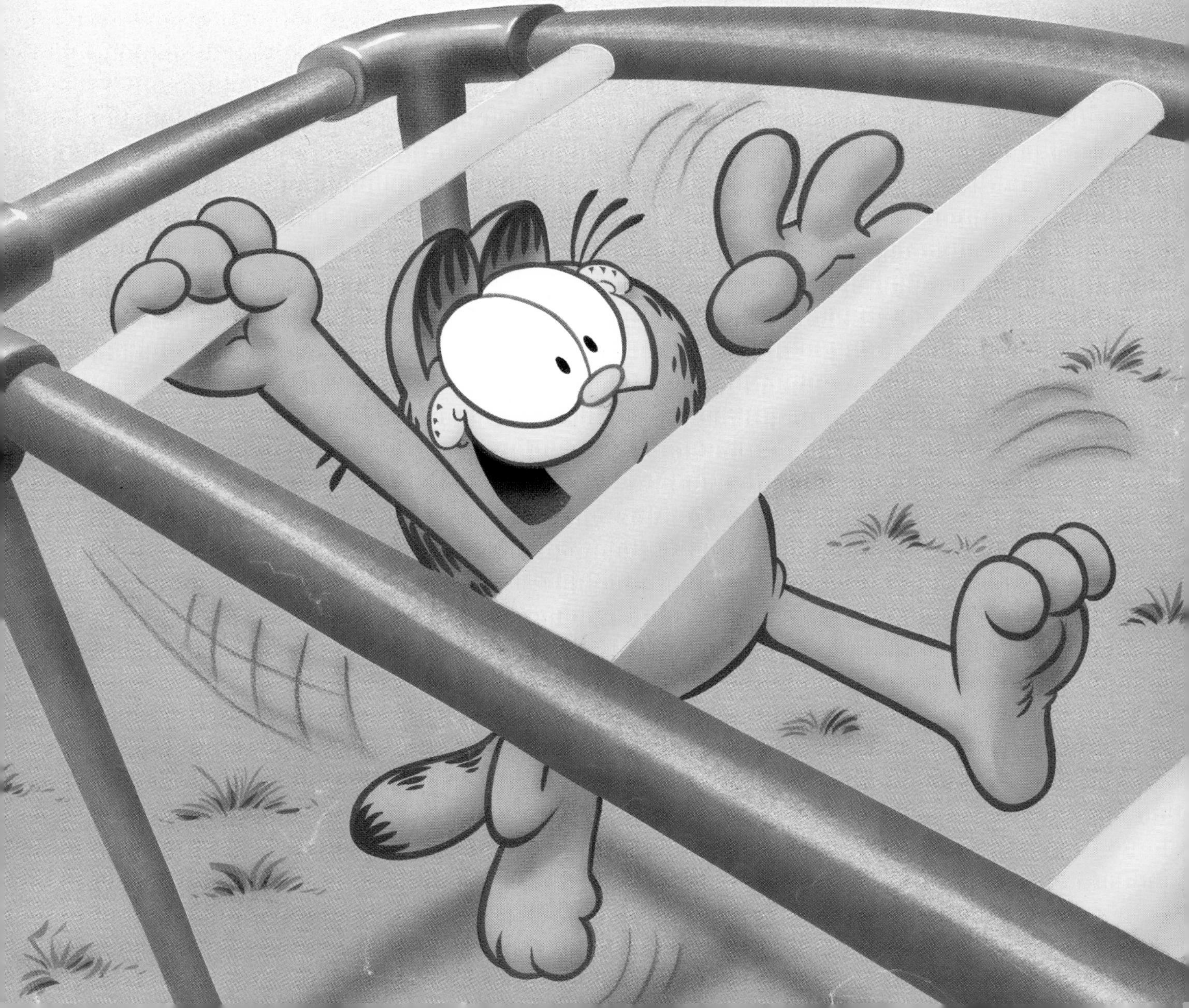

STUPID CUPID

Cupid was in a hurry. He had wasted an hour bouncing love arrows off a grouchy lawyer. Now he was late for his other Valentine's Day appointments. And if he did not fire his arrows at the precise place and time, then many love-starved creatures would miss their chance for romance. So when the winged boy encountered a little turbulence at 5,000 feet, he was too distracted to notice one of his arrows slip out of his quiver and spiral toward a park below.

Odie heard a whistling sound, then a "thunk" as the arrow struck the ground. He looked up, but saw only clouds. Cocking his head, he stared at the arrow. He circled it. He sniffed. He barked. Finally, he pulled the arrow from the ground, and trotted off to find Garfield.

He discovered Garfield sprawled on a park bench, enjoying the unusually mild February day. Odie dropped the arrow at Garfield's feet. He barked once.

"Go away, Odie," said Garfield.

Odie barked again. Garfield frowned and raised his eyelids.

"Where did you get the arrow?" he asked.

Odie pointed to the sky.

"Maybe a robin dropped it," said Garfield. "Yeah, Robin *Hood*! Get it?"

Odie just stared.

Garfield sighed. "Dumb jokes are wasted on the *really* dumb," he said. "Okay, let's take a closer look."

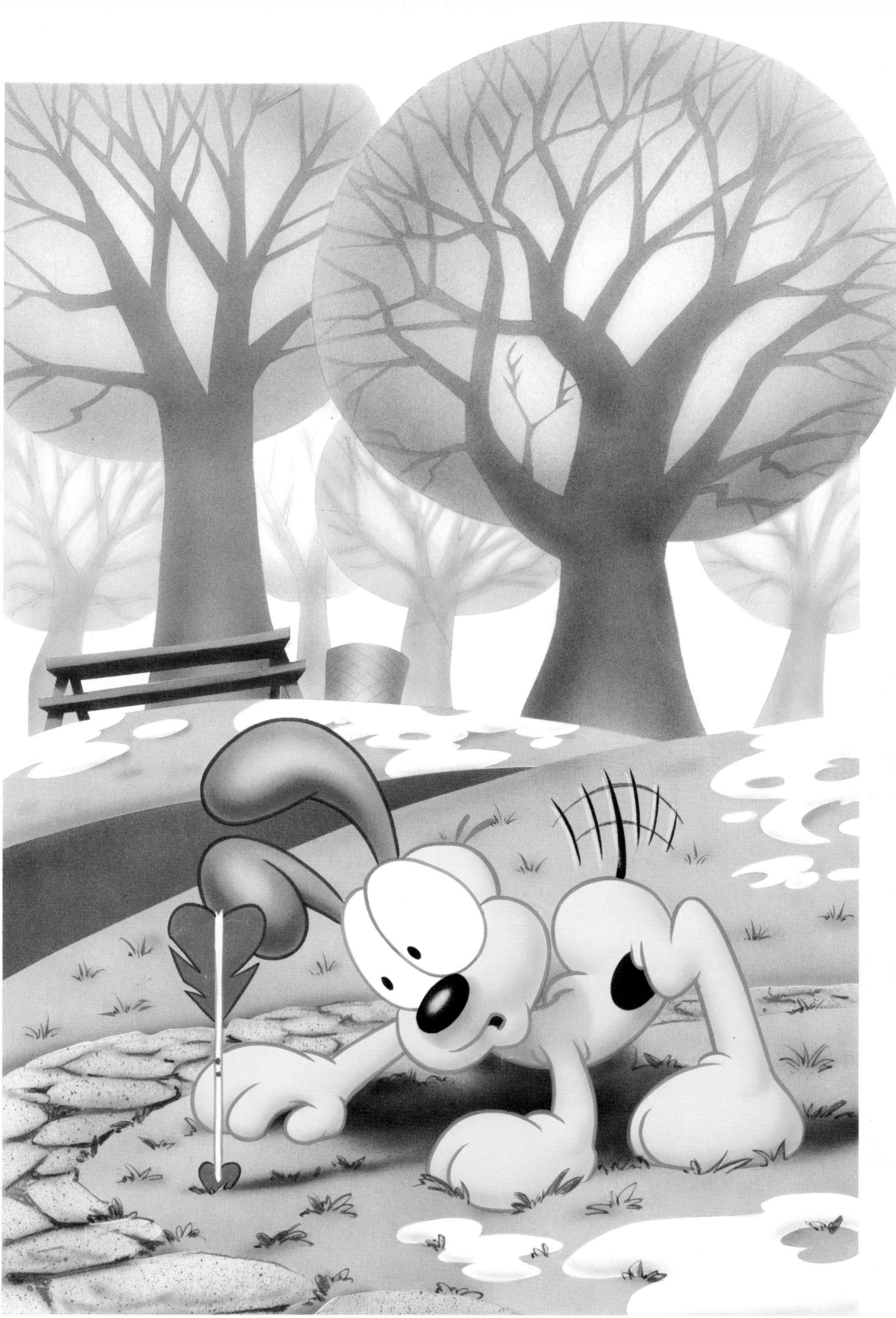

Garfield studied the arrow. "The shaft says 'Warning: For Cupid's Bow Only.' And look at these little hearts. Hey! Wait a minute! Odie, do you know what this is?"

Odie shook his head.

"Today is Valentine's Day, right? This must be one of Cupid's arrows! We've got the power of love right here in our paws! With this, I'll be irresistible! And you'll be somewhat less repulsive!"

Just then a lovely female feline came strolling down the path.

"Here's the first lucky lady," said Garfield. "You take the arrow. I'll look adorable. When she notices me — and they *always* notice me — you zing her with the arrow."

Odie nodded and crouched behind the bench.

The female cat approached. Garfield smiled. "Hey, gorgeous," he said. "How would you like a date with the 'Round Mound of Romance'?"

The cat turned to Garfield and made a sour face.

"Now, Odie!" cried Garfield.

Odie hurled the arrow at the lady cat. Unfortunately, Odie's aim was as lame as his brain. The arrow sailed far over the cat and disappeared behind a hedge.

"Ouch!" cried a female voice from behind the hedge.

"I don't like the sound of that," said Garfield.

The next moment a large female dog bounded out from behind the hedge.

"And I *really* don't like the looks of that," added Garfield.

Brandishing the arrow, the dog marched up to Garfield. "Does this belong to you?" she growled. "Because if it does, I'm going to . . . I'm going to . . ."

"Forget the whole thing?" suggested Garfield.

A strange light appeared in the dog's eyes. "Why, I'm going to give you a great big hug!" She dropped the arrow and threw her arms around Garfield.

"Odie, you stupid Cupid!" cried Garfield. "Look at the love mess you've made!"

Odie picked up the arrow and shrugged apologetically.

"Kiss me, you handsome hunk of cat hair!" demanded the dog.

"No way!" replied Garfield. "Lips that touch dog food will never touch mine!" With that he wriggled out of the dog's embrace and raced away.

"Come back!" called the dog. "I want you for my little love pumpkin!"

Garfield ran for his life, the dog ran after Garfield, and Odie ran after them both. All around the park they raced — up and down slides, over and under swings, in and out of the monkey bars. But the dog refused to give up.

"You're so cute when you're sweaty!" she called to Garfield.

"Just my luck," gasped Garfield. "I finally meet someone who's crazy about me, and she turns out to be a real dog!"

Finally Garfield scampered up the seesaw. His weight tilted the board, causing him to slide down the other side. At that moment the dog leaped onto the opposite end of the seesaw, driving it toward the ground and catapulting Garfield high into the air! He landed — WHOOMP! — in a tree.

"Well, every relationship has its ups and downs," moaned Garfield.

Unable to climb the tree, the dog circled beneath Garfield, barking declarations of love at the beleaguered fat cat.

"Come down," she called. "I can't live without you!"

"Neither can I," Garfield replied. "But it wouldn't work out. I have charm and intelligence, and you have . . . dog breath."

At that moment Cupid fluttered down beside Garfield.

"It seems we have a situation here," Cupid observed.

"We certainly do," Garfield replied. "Thanks to your lost arrow and my idiot assistant over there." Garfield pointed at Odie, who smiled and waved the arrow.

"Aha! You found it!" said Cupid. "And I'll bet you tried it out too."

"I swear, I didn't know the arrow was loaded," Garfield declared.

"Which explains why that dog is hopelessly in love with you."

"Can you do anything about that?" asked Garfield.

"Well, it looks like the arrow only nicked her," said Cupid. "So the infatuation will probably wear off in a week or so."

"A week! She'll hug me to a pulp by then!"

"Don't sweat it," Cupid replied. "I also carry special 'love anti-dote arrows' for correcting mistakes like this." He drew an arrow from his quiver and fitted it to the bow. "One shot and your date with Rover will be over."

Cupid pointed his bow at the dog, who gazed lovingly at Garfield.

"Ta-ta," said Garfield. "Let's not do this again sometime."

"My owner is the head chef at an Italian restaurant," said the dog. "We could make beautiful pasta together."

"Hold the arrow!" cried Garfield, grabbing Cupid's arm.

"But I have to shoot the dog with the antidote," Cupid argued.

"Over my full tummy!" said Garfield. "I can see now that this is a case of true love."

"It is?"

"Yes, she truly loves me . . . and I truly love Italian food."

Garfield slid down the tree trunk and offered his paws to the dog.

"I knew you'd come down," she said. "You're so considerate."

"That's true," said Garfield. "But let's not talk about me. Let's talk about tonight's menu."

And so, as Odie and Cupid shook their heads, Garfield and his main mutt walked off paw-in-paw.

Of course, one week later they were fighting like cats and dogs.

GARFIELD'S SUMMER LOVE

"Here we are," said Jon to Garfield and Odie as they drove up to their cabin. "Our vacation destination — that famed resort, the Catskill Mountains."

"With a name like that, I like it already," said Garfield.

"Isn't it inspiring?" commented Jon, marvelling at the scenery. "The glistening lakes, the majestic mountains . . ."

"The barbecue pits," added Garfield, spying a nearby picnic area. "Now that's what I call inspiring!"

Suddenly, something caught Garfield's eye. It was a female cat strolling by. A gorgeous female cat, no less.

"Check out that fine feline," cooed Garfield, elbowing Odie. "She's adorable. I'm adorable. Obviously we're compatible."

Garfield tried to whistle, but he was too nervous. Instead, he just drooled.

Odie grinned and shook his head. He knew that look in Garfield's eyes. It was the look of love — a look normally reserved for lasagna.

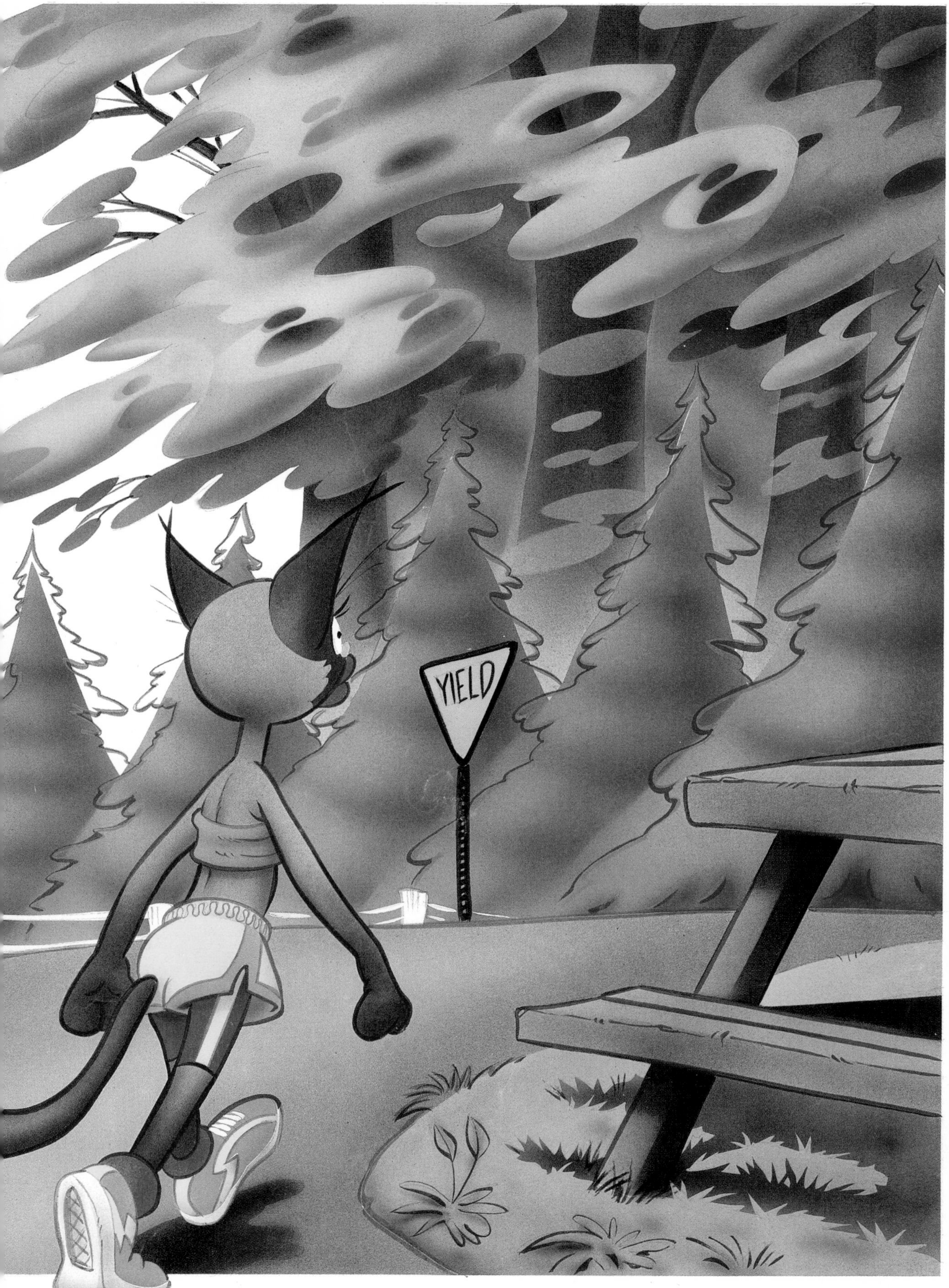
YIELD

That night in the dining hall, as Garfield stuffed his face, thoughts of the pretty kitty filled his head. Then, across the crowded room, he saw her.

"It's fate! She and me . . . it's meant to be," mused Garfield, waxing poetic.

His heart began to pound. His paws began to sweat. It was now or never. He *had* to get her attention.

"**B-U-R-P**!"

A thunderous burp echoed through the hall. All eyes turned to Garfield.

"Garfield!" exclaimed Jon. "That's embarrassing!"

"Thanks for pointing out the obvious," muttered Garfield, blushing. "Well, at least now she knows I'm alive."

Garfield decided to make his move. He slipped away from the table and boldly introduced himself to the object of his desire.

"Hi, I'm Gargoyle," he babbled. "Uh — I mean, Garfield. Anyway, about that burp . . . that wasn't really me. Jon, my owner, he's a ventriloquist with a gross sense of humor."

"Oh, that's good to hear," she said. "If there's one thing I can't stand, it's bad manners. By the way, my name is Violet . . . like the flower."

"Some of my tastiest snacks have been flowers," gushed Garfield.

"Oh, you're so funny," said Violet with a chuckle.

YES! thought Garfield. *She thinks I'm funny. And I didn't even have to put on my plastic antlers.*

"Excuse me," said Violet, interrupting Garfield's thoughts. "I have to go now, but maybe we could get together tomorrow?"

"Cool," replied Garfield. "We could gobble till we wobble at the smorgasbord brunch."

Garfield, trying to put his best paw forward, winced as the awkward words slipped out. However, Violet did not take him seriously.

"You and your crazy sense of humor," she giggled. "I thought we could watch the sunrise, then go for a jog. Do you like to jog?"

"Running is my life," boasted Garfield. *Especially to the refrigerator,* he added to himself.

"Great," said Violet. "Then I'll meet you by the lake tomorrow at the crack of dawn."

"I must be cracked to get up at dawn," mumbled Garfield.

Early the next morning, Garfield met Violet by the lake. She was bright-eyed and bushy-tailed. He was bleary-eyed and just plain bushed.

"Isn't the sunrise glorious?" observed Violet.

"Yeah, it's great," yawned Garfield. "I just wish we had taped it and watched it later."

"Always the cut-up," said Violet. "Shall we start jogging?"

For a moment, Garfield considered refusing.

This goes against everything I stand for, he thought.

But then Garfield looked into Violet's big beautiful eyes and knew he could refuse her nothing.

"Let's do it," he nodded reluctantly.

As they ran, they talked. Actually, Violet talked while Garfield just huffed and puffed. She told him about her life and her interests.

" . . . and two of my favorite things are exercising and reading poetry," said Violet.

Garfield flinched at the thought.

"But I must admit," continued Violet, "that I do enjoy snacking in front of the TV."

Garfield heaved a big sigh of relief.

"Yes, there's nothing like chomping on a crisp tossed salad while watching a good documentary," added Violet.

Garfield's heart sank.

This relationship is doomed, he thought. *She's into fitness and I'm into fatness. Isn't there anything we have in common?*

Then Garfield had a stroke of inspiration.

"Do you like spiders?" he asked.

"Heavens, no!" shrieked Violet.

I knew it! thought Garfield. *We are compatible. We might just make it after all.*

Soon they finished their run.

"Care to join me for some fresh fruit?" asked Violet.

"Uh, I can't," said Garfield as visions of donuts danced in his head. "Jon's expecting me. Can we meet tonight — like maybe *after* dinner?"

"Perfect," replied Violet. "There's an 'opera on the green' tonight. Arias under the stars . . . how romantic!"

How strange, thought Garfield. *The same country that invented lasagna gave us opera. Go figure.*

"Until tonight," said Violet, jogging away.

"Until then," said Garfield, waving good-bye. *Boy,* he thought, *the things we do for love.*

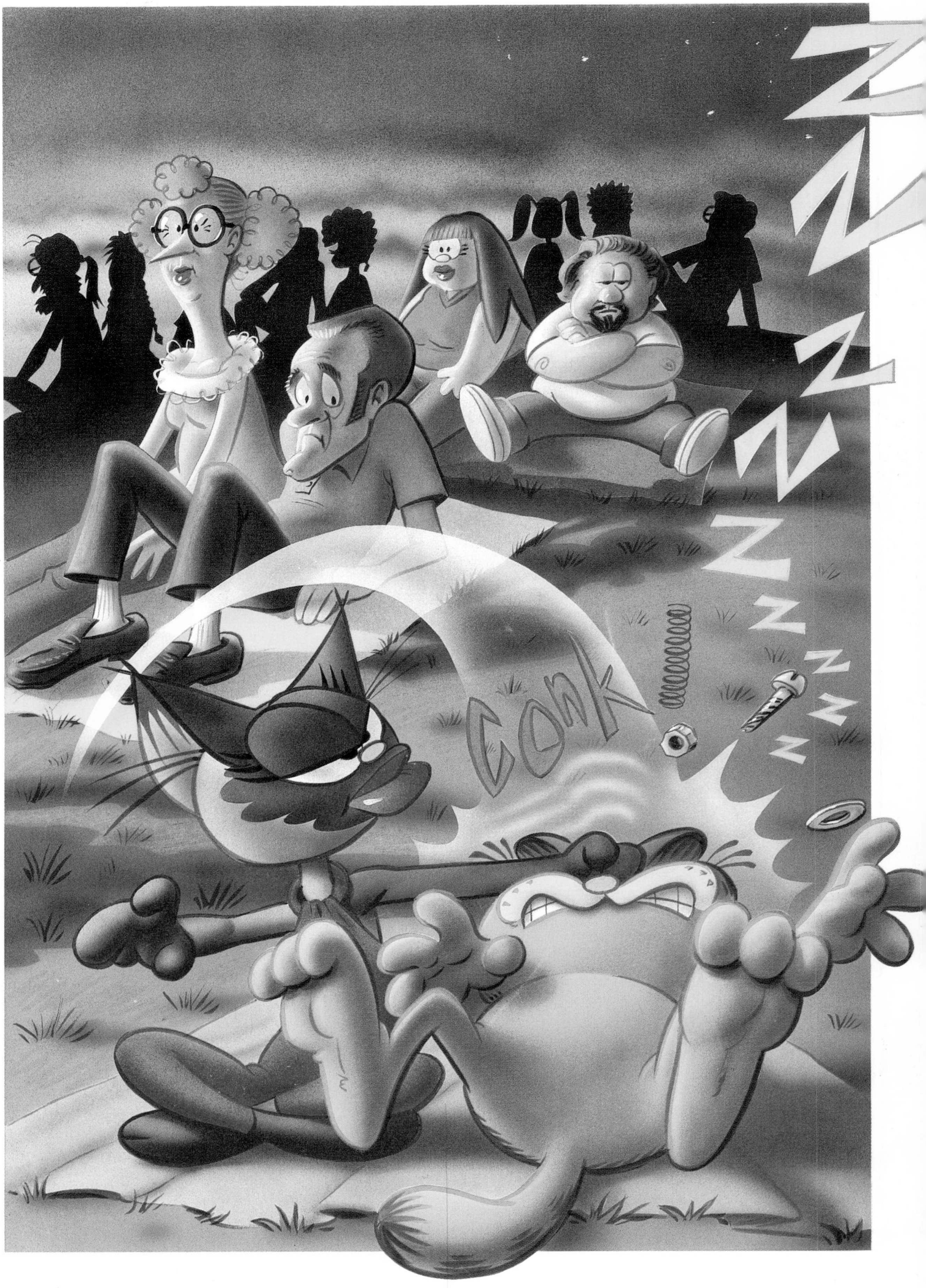
ZZZZZZZZZZZ
CONK

Garfield spent the day pigging out so his appetite would be under control that night. By the time he met Violet for the opera, he was stuffed.

Now I'm sure to be the perfect gentlecat, thought Garfield.

The opera began. Music filled the air. The stars twinkled and so did Violet's eyes. Everything was perfect. Suddenly, the romantic mood was shattered by what sounded like a jackhammer. But it wasn't a jackhammer — it was Garfield snoring!

"Wake up," whispered Violet, nudging Garfield.

But the snoozemeister snored on.

"Garfield!" snapped Violet, conking him on the noggin.

"Huh?" spluttered Garfield. "Where are we?"

"We're at the opera," said Violet, "and I need to talk with you."

They hurried out to a spot where they could talk.

"I'm sorry," said Garfield. "I didn't mean to embarrass you."

"That's okay," said Violet. "I figured you weren't an opera buff when you asked me where the hot-dog vendors were. What I wanted to say is that I have to go back home tomorrow. I wanted to tell you before, but I didn't want to ruin our fun."

When Garfield heard that Violet was leaving, a strange feeling swept over him. It was a feeling of relief.

"We'll never see each other again," said Violet.

Garfield didn't know what to say. Finally, Violet leaned over and gave him a kiss.

"Good-bye, my crazy cat."

As Garfield stood there alone with his thoughts, something became clear. *I can't be happy if I can't be myself. Violet was nice, but she wasn't my type. And I wasn't her type, either. From now on, I've got to be me. And why not? I'm too cool to be anyone else!*

RACING REX

Garfield stepped out his front door and looked around. "What a beautiful day!" he said. "The sun is shining. The birds are singing. Arlene is walking by, holding hands with some strange cat . . . Hey! What's going on here? Arlene!"

"Oh. Hello, Garfield," said Arlene. "This is my new and *very close friend* Rex. Rex, this is Garfield."

"Nice to meet you," said Rex.

"Don't count on it," Garfield replied.

"Rex and I met two days ago," Arlene said, "and we've barely been apart since then. Rex is *very* considerate. Do you know what I mean, Garfield? No, I don't suppose you do.

"Rex is a famous Hollywood stunt cat," Arlene continued. "He performs all the dangerous tricks the actor cats can't do. He once jumped off a burning bridge into a river full of crocodiles!"

"Big deal," said Garfield. "I once dove into a pile of Jon's dirty socks. That took *real* guts!"

"And Rex is so strong," said Arlene, squeezing the stranger's arm. "Stunt cats have to be in great shape. That's another thing *you* wouldn't know anything about."

"There's nothing wrong with my shape!" snapped Garfield.

"He's right," said Rex. "His shape is perfect . . . for a basketball!"

Garfield tried to stick out his chest, but somehow it slid down into his tummy. "Listen, Rocks —"

"It's Rex," said Arlene.

"Listen, Rats," hissed Garfield. "I'll match my shape against yours anytime!"

"Garfield, I think you're jealous!" said Arlene.

"Jealous?" said Rex. "He looks more like *jelly* to me."

"You're asking for it, Rugs," Garfield snapped. "Someday I'm going to teach you a lesson."

"How about today?" Rex replied. "How about now? Come on. We'll see who's in better shape. I'll race you around the block."

"Uh, I can't right now," said Garfield.

"Why not?"

"Uh, because I, uh . . . I have to wash my teddy bear."

"I thought so," said Rex.

"But I'll be ready to race tomorrow morning!"

"I'll be here," said Rex. Then he tucked Arlene under his arm and jogged away.

"I can't believe Arlene is attracted to that muscle head," muttered Garfield. "But I'll show her who's the top cat around here!"

Garfield began training for the race. First, he tried to do a push-up. But he couldn't get up, no matter how hard he pushed!

Then he tried a pull-up. But instead of Garfield going up, the pull-up bar came down!

So he decided to try some long-distance running. But in Garfield's case, a long distance was about ten feet. He quickly collapsed, and Odie had to carry him into the house.

"It's . . . no . . . use," Garfield gasped. "You can't turn fatness into fitness overnight. I'll have to rely on my brains."

Early the next morning Garfield, Odie, Arlene, and Rex met in front of Garfield's house.

"The rules of this race are simple," Arlene explained. "You must race all the way around the block. First one back to this spot — that would be you, Rex — is the winner."

Rex shook Garfield's hand. "I hope you'll be a good loser," Rex said.

"You can show me how," Garfield replied.

"On your marks!" shouted Arlene. Rex crouched like an Olympic sprinter. Garfield stood with his arms folded.

"Get set! GO!"

Rex raced away. Garfield didn't move.

"Giving up already?" asked Arlene.

"Just watch!" said Garfield. "Odie, it's time for plan A."

Odie handed Garfield a pair of springs. Garfield attached the springs to his feet. SPROING! Garfield bounced over Arlene's head.

"That's cheating!" cried Arlene.

"You said we had to race around the block. But you never said we had to *run!*"

SPROING! SPROING! Garfield bounced down the block. SPRO-ING! SPROING! SPROING!

THUNK! Garfield dangled high above the ground, a tree limb clenched between his teeth. *There's too much "SPROING" in these springs,* thought Garfield. *I'd better switch to plan B.*

Quickly Garfield laced on a pair of roller blades. Then he grabbed Odie by the tail, and shouted, "Let's roll!"

Odie sped along the sidewalk with Garfield rolling right behind. "Go, Odie, go!" cried Garfield. Odie's ears flapped in the breeze. His tongue waved wildly.

Rounding a corner, Garfield spotted Rex not far ahead. "We're going to pass him, Odie!" cried Garfield. "Nothing can stop us now!"

Nothing . . . except Odie's tongue, which suddenly wrapped around Odie's eyes, causing the perplexed pup to veer out of control.

"Abandon dog!" shouted Garfield. He let go of Odie's tail . . . and rocketed across the street, through a fence, over a hedge, and into a mailbox!

"Oooo, I think I broke myself," moaned Garfield. "Time for — ouch! — plan C."

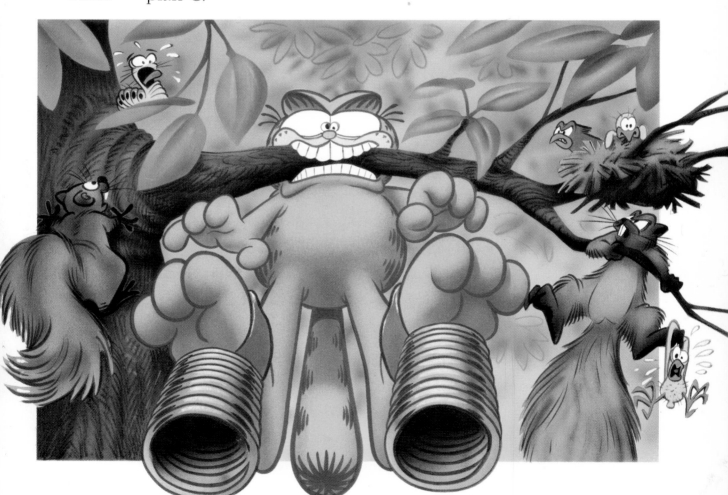

Garfield cut through the yards until he reached a house on the opposite side of the block. In the front yard a fierce dog sat chained to a post.

Garfield looked down the block. There was Rex, jogging confidently.

"Hey, dog!" said Garfield. "See that cat? He says you couldn't catch a slow kitten."

"GROWRRR!" replied the dog, pulling on his chain.

"He says you're a walking flea resort."

The dog snarled louder and clawed at the dirt.

"He says your mother was pound scum."

"GROWRRRRRR!" roared the dog. With a violent jerk he snapped the chain, sprang over the fence, and raced toward Rex.

"Happy chomping!" Garfield called after him.

A few minutes later Garfield danced across the finish line.

"I don't believe it!" cried Arlene. "What happened to Rex?"

"The last time I saw him, he was showing a very angry dog how a stunt cat climbs a telephone pole."

"Why was the dog so mad at Rex?"

Garfield shrugged. "Maybe it was something he said."

Arlene placed her paw on Garfield's arm. "To be honest, Garfield, I was never really interested in Rex. I just thought if I gave Rex a little attention, *you* might pay a little more attention to *me*."

"Arlene, Arlene," said Garfield. "Just because I ignore you constantly doesn't mean I don't care."

"It doesn't?"

"Of course not," said Garfield. "After all, you and I have something very special in common."

"What's that?" asked Arlene.

"We're both wild about *me*!"

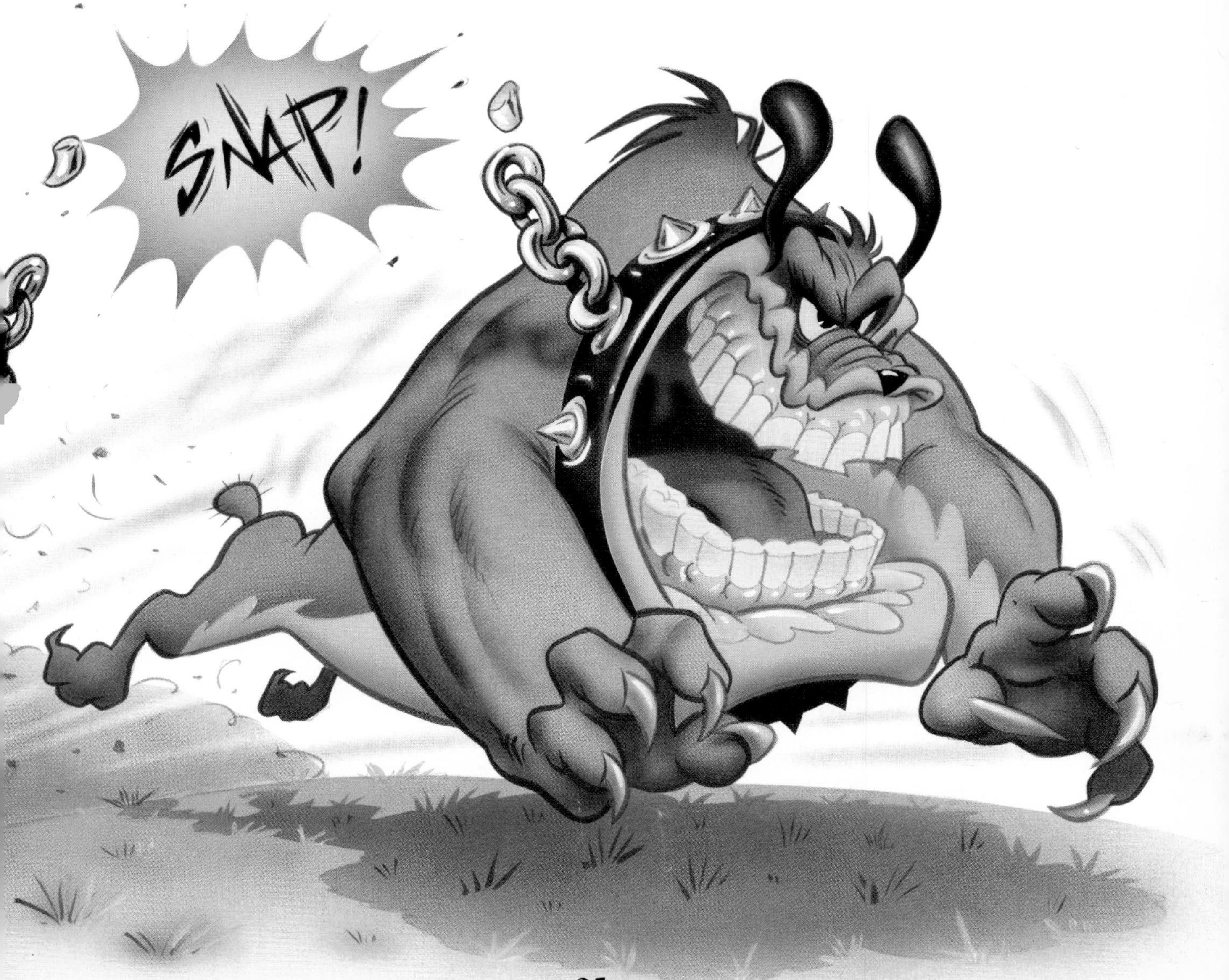
SNAP!

JON'S DATE WITH DESTINY

"Check out these books," said Garfield as he motioned Odie toward the small bookcase in Jon's bedroom. *Organizing Your Sock Drawer, Kissing Made Simple, Antiques for Geeks.* Boy, you can tell a lot about people from the books they read. Jon's almost as clueless as you are."

"Hunh?" replied Odie, obviously puzzled.

"I rest my case," said Garfield. Then something caught his eye. "Hey, here's a book about hypnosis! Now that's more like it."

Garfield hopped on Jon's bed and began reading. Odie scrambled up beside him.

"Listen up, you doofus dog. You might learn something," instructed Garfield. "According to this book, almost anyone can be hypnotized. That's when you put someone in a trance and then control his mind. Of course, it would never work on you. First you have to *have* a mind."

Odie stuck out his tongue at Garfield. Just then, Jon strolled into the room whistling a merry tune. "I've got a date tonight, boys," he proudly announced as he looked in the dresser mirror and adjusted his tie.

"With a fashion consultant, I hope," said Garfield, as he critically eyed Jon's yellow suit covered with red polka dots.

"How do I look?" he asked, modeling his outfit.

"Like a canary with measles," cracked Garfield. He elbowed Odie, who began to snicker. "Is this a date or an audition for the circus?"

Jon continued to admire himself in front of the mirror. Flexing his puny muscles, he spoke to his reflection. "Arbuckle, you're a Greek god."

"Make that a *geek* god," countered Garfield, disgustedly shaking his head. "Jon's hopeless, Odie. He's such a loser, he can't even get a good-night kiss from his mom. If only he had *my* hypnotic personality, he'd be a major babe magnet. For once, he might actually get a *second* date with the same woman."

Odie rolled his eyes in response to Garfield's bragging. Suddenly, Garfield sprang to his feet.

"Hey, that gives me an idea!" he exclaimed. "I'll hypnotize Jon and give him my irresistible personality. Look, I can use this," he said, picking up a sock that was peeking out from under the bed. Garfield scurried across the room and climbed atop the dresser. Dangling the sock in front of Jon's face, he slowly swung it back and forth, back and forth.

"Hey, that's my missing sock," said Jon. "Where did you . . ." Jon's voice faded as his eyes began to blink.

"You are getting sleepy, very *sleeeepy*," said Garfield, swinging the sock to and fro until Jon's eyes had closed completely. "I think it worked, Odie," whispered Garfield. "I think Jon's in a trance. Let's test him to make sure.

"Jon, you are now under my control. If you understand, act like a dog."

"Ribbit! Ribbit!" croaked Jon as he hopped around the room.

"I said a *dog*, not a *frog*," said Garfield.

"ARF!" barked Jon, sniffing and scratching and running around in circles.

"That's a dog, all right," said Garfield. "But you won't be a dog — or a dweeb — for long. Now listen closely, Jon. During your date tonight, you will *not* be your usual nerdy self. Instead, you will be witty. You will be charming. You will be *me!* I hereby 'Garfieldize' your personality. No longer are you the 'Duke of Dork.' From this moment on you are 'Jon Juan, the King of Hearts.' What do you say to that?"

"Feed me," replied Jon. "The way to my heart is through my stomach."

"My thoughts exactly," agreed Garfield. "Why, if you weren't you, I'd swear you were me."

"What's with this clown suit?" complained Jon, looking at his clothes with a new eye. "This date deserves my orange suit with the black stripes. I feel like a tiger tonight."

"Or at least a very cool cat," said Garfield, smiling proudly at his creation.

Jon quickly changed clothes and headed for the door — the refrigerator door.

"Nothing like a little appetizer before dinner," he said as he gobbled a turkey leg. "Too bad I don't have time for a nap."

Jon flung away the devoured drumstick and ambled out to his car.

"I've got a date with destiny," he yelled. "Don't wait up."

"Have fun, Romeo," said Garfield. "And don't do anything I wouldn't do!"

A short time later, Jon arrived at the restaurant where he had arranged to meet his date, Tish. She was waiting impatiently at a table.

"Jon Arbuckle, you're thirty minutes late!" said Tish.

"The good things in life are worth waiting for," replied Jon. "Besides, I have a good excuse. I had to stop at the dog pound."

"Really?" asked Tish. "Why?"

"To pound the dogs, of course!" answered Jon, howling with laughter.

Tish gave Jon a strange look.

"Speaking of dogs," he said, "I'm ready to sink my teeth into a big juicy hot dog."

"But Jon," said Tish, "this is a seafood restaurant."

"I see the food," said Jon, pointing to a dessert cart across the room, "and now I'm going to eat it!"

Jon bolted toward the food, but Tish grabbed him by the arm.

"Are you out of your mind?" she said. "Sit down until the waiter takes our order."

"If I must," grumbled Jon, pouting. "But do you mind if I watch TV while we wait?" he asked as he removed a hand-held television from his jacket pocket. "It's time for my favorite show, *Bowling for Donuts*."

"Yes, I do mind," said Tish. "That's incredibly rude. You're supposed to be paying attention to *me*."

"I'm sorry," said Jon. "Of course I'd rather look at you. You're very pretty."

Tish smiled grudgingly.

"Really, I like everything about you," continued Jon, turning on the charm. "Your fiery red lips, like zesty tomato sauce . . . your alluring eyes, like two meatballs in a plate of spaghetti . . . your —"

"Enough already," interrupted Tish. "Is this a date or a feeding frenzy? What's wrong with you? You didn't act like this when we met at the gym."

"The gym?" groaned Jon. "I'll join a gym when they put in a bakery! Just the thought of working out makes me tired," he added, yawning and slumping down in his seat. "My idea of exercise is a marathon snoozzzzze . . ."

Later that night Jon, still hypnotized, returned home. He was eagerly greeted by Garfield and Odie.

"All hail the 'King of Hearts" proclaimed Garfield. "Well, how did it go? As if I need to ask. I'll bet she was putty in your paws."

"It was the strangest thing," said Jon. "I apparently dozed off. When the waiter woke me up, he told me that Tish had stormed out of the restaurant, saying that she never wanted to see me again. I can't imagine why."

"I know why," said Garfield. "The hypnosis must have worn off." Garfield snapped his fingers in disgust. "Your sizzle has fizzled and now you're as nerdy as ever."

By snapping his fingers, Garfield unintentionally snapped Jon out of his trance. Jon would never recall the events of the evening. He was now, indeed, as nerdy as ever.

"Hmmm . . . what should I do?" wondered Jon. "Should I sort my socks, or dust the ceiling tiles? Maybe I'll crawl into my jammies and listen to a little bagpipe music. I could take a bubble bath. Of course, that always makes me seasick . . ."

"Jon belongs on the cover of *Dorks Illustrated*," said Garfield to Odie. "No wonder his date was a disaster. If only I could have gone in his place. Then Tish would have been the one who was mesmerized!"